Mood Board Pages for Inter...

An Interior Design Portfolio Organizer Journal
(Portrait Format)

VIRGINIA I SMITH

VIRYABOS
CREATIONS
INTERIOR DESIGNER

- Images used under license by 123rf.com

Thank you for your purchase

We hope you enjoy using this interior design workbook. If there is anything you feel may be great to add (or remove), please don't hesitate to leave a comment or a review.

Shop our other interior design-related workbooks and activity sketchbooks, planners, journals, and business books created specifically for interior designers and students of interior design: https://www.amazon.com/-/e/B07ZPHJD8R

Virginia I Smith **Brand Logo**

Blog: https://simpleinteriorconcepts.blogspot.com/

Related Books

ASIN: B09FS2TLF2

ASIN: B09VLWST7B

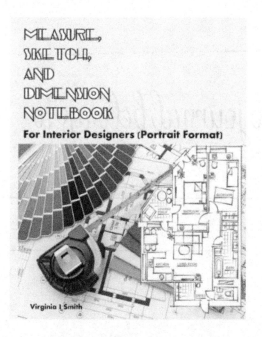

ASIN: B08F6CGC5M

ASIN: B08KH3R53Q

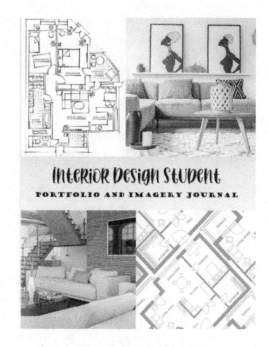

ASIN: B08BRKDYTV

ASIN: B09P25L85D

This mood board portfolio journal belongs to

_____

_____

Contact:

_____

_____

_____

_____

_____

Inspiration

Mood

Style

Inspiration

_____

_____

_____

_____

_____

_____

_____

_____

_____

_____

_____

_____

_____

_____

_____

_____

_____

_____

_____

_____

_____

_____

Colors & Tones

Vendors & Suppliers

Inspiration

Inspiration

Colors & Tones

Swatches & Textures

Vendors & Suppliers

Notes & Statements

Mood

Style

Mood

Style

Inspiration

Colors & Tones

Swatches & Textures

Vendors & Suppliers

Mood

Style

Inspiration

Mood

Style

Inspiration

Colors & Tones

Vendors & Suppliers

Mood

Style

Inspiration

Mood

Style

Inspiration

Colors & Tones

Vendors & Suppliers

Notes & Statements

Mood

Style

Inspiration

Mood

Style

Inspiration

Colors & Tones

Swatches & Textures

Vendors & Suppliers

Mood

Style

Mood

Style

Inspiration

Colors & Tones

Vendors & Suppliers

Notes & Statements

Mood

Style

Inspiration

Mood

Style

Colors & Tones

Swatches & Textures

Notes & Statements

Mood

Style

Inspiration

Mood

Style

Inspiration

Colors & Tones

Swatches & Textures

Vendors & Suppliers

Mood

Style

Inspiration

Mood

Style

Inspiration

Colors & Tones

Swatches & Textures

Vendors & Suppliers

Mood

Style

Inspiration

Mood

Style

Inspiration

Colors & Tones

Swatches & Textures

Vendors & Suppliers

Notes & Statements

Mood

Style

Inspiration

Mood   Style

96

Colors & Tones

Vendors & Suppliers

Mood   Style

Inspiration

Mood

Style

Inspiration

Colors & Tones

Vendors & Suppliers

Notes & Statements

Inspiration

Mood

Style

Colors & Tones

Swatches & Textures

Vendors & Suppliers

Mood

Style

120

Mood

Style

Colors & Tones

Vendors & Suppliers

Mood

Style

Inspiration

Mood

Style

Colors & Tones

Swatches & Textures

Vendors & Suppliers

Notes & Statements

Mood

Style

Inspiration

Mood

Style

Inspiration

Colors & Tones

Swatches & Textures

Vendors & Suppliers

Mood

Style

Inspiration

Mood

Style

Colors & Tones

Swatches & Textures

Vendors & Suppliers

Mood

Style

Inspiration

Colors & Tones

Swatches & Textures

Vendors & Suppliers

Mood

Style

Mood

Style

Inspiration

Colors & Tones

Swatches & Textures

Vendors & Suppliers

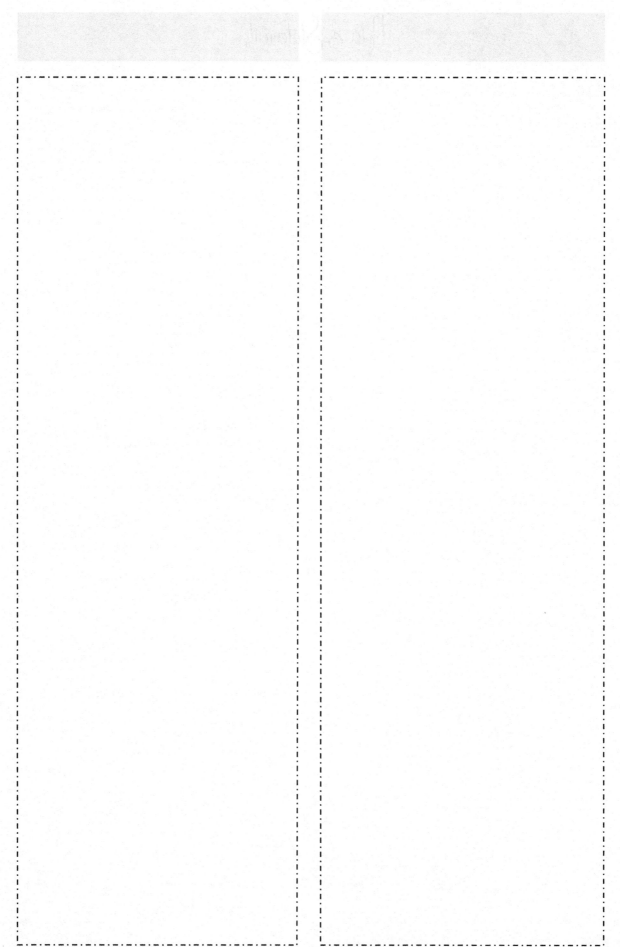

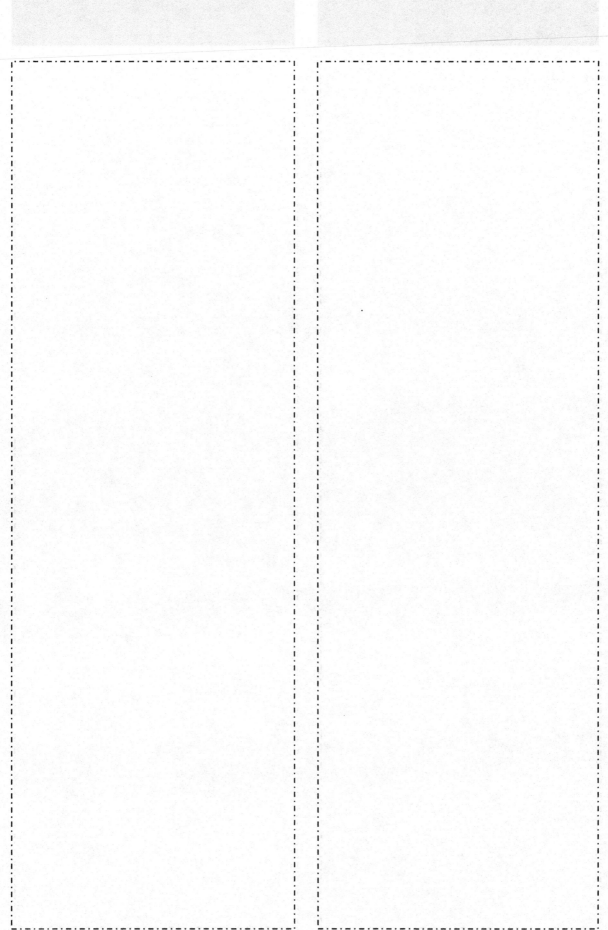

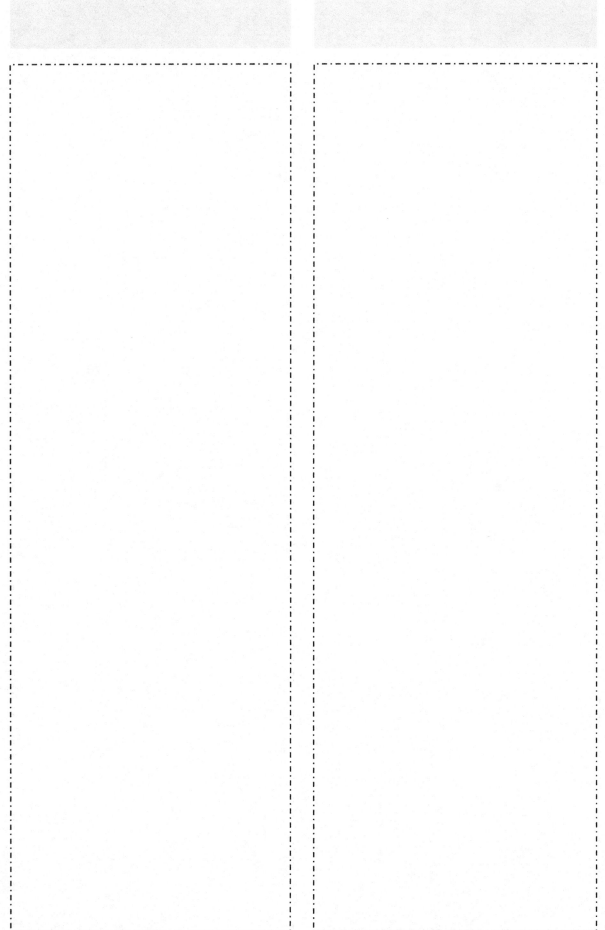

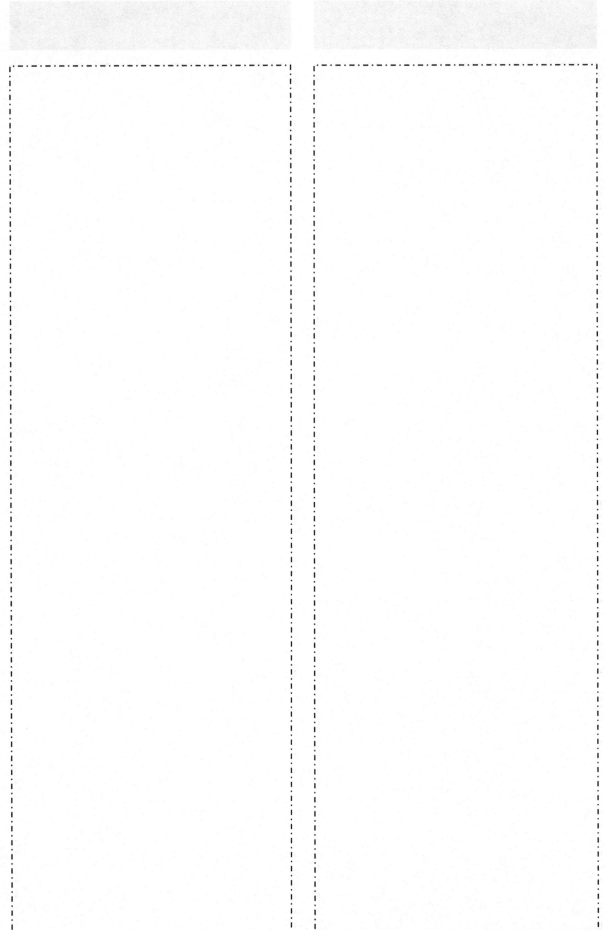

Index

Date	Project	Page

Index

Date	Project	Page

Index

Date	Project	Page

Index

Date	Project	Page

Made in the USA
Monee, IL
05 September 2024

65195316R00098